JIGSAW

by Lee Coffey

|| SAMUEL FRENCH ||

FOR AMATEUR PRODUCTION ENQUIRIES

UNITED KINGDOM AND WORLD
EXCLUDING NORTH AMERICA
licensing@concordtheatricals.co.uk
020-7054-7298

Each title is subject to availability from Concord Theatricals, depending upon country of performance.

---

written permission of the publisher. No one shall share this title, or part of this title, to any social media or file hosting websites.

The moral right of Lee Coffey to be identified as author of this work has been asserted in accordance with Section 77 of the Copyright, Designs and Patents Act 1988.

USE OF COPYRIGHTED MUSIC

A licence issued by Concord Theatricals to perform this play does not include permission to use the incidental music specified in this publication. In the United Kingdom: Where the place of performance is already licensed by the PERFORMING RIGHT SOCIETY (PRS) a return of the music used must be made to them. If the place of performance is not so licensed then application should be made to PRS for Music (www.prsformusic.com). A separate and additional licence from PHONOGRAPHIC PERFORMANCE LTD (www.ppluk.com) may be needed whenever commercial recordings are used. Outside the United Kingdom: Please contact the appropriate music licensing authority in your territory for the rights to any incidental music.

USE OF COPYRIGHTED THIRD-PARTY MATERIALS

Licensees are solely responsible for obtaining formal written permission from copyright owners to use copyrighted third-party materials (e.g., artworks, logos) in the performance of this play and are strongly cautioned to do so. If no such permission is obtained by the licensee, then the licensee must use only original materials that the licensee owns and controls. Licensees are solely responsible and liable for clearances of all third-party copyrighted materials, and shall indemnify the copyright owners of the play(s) and their licensing agent, Concord Theatricals Ltd., against any costs, expenses, losses and liabilities arising from the use of such copyrighted third-party materials by licensees.

IMPORTANT BILLING AND CREDIT REQUIREMENTS

If you have obtained performance rights to this title, please refer to your licensing agreement for important billing and credit requirements.

NOTE

This edition reflects a rehearsal draft of the script and may differ from the final production.

JIGSAW was commissioned and originally produced by Glass Mask Theatre, with support from The Arts Council of Ireland, and premiered at Glass Mask Theatre in Dublin on 6 May 2025. The cast and creative team were as follows:

OLDER . . . . Alan Devine
YOUNGER . . . . Craig Connolly

Writer . . . . Lee Coffey
Director . . . . Ian Toner
Creative Director . . . . Rex Ryan
Creative Producer . . . . Migle Ryan
Set Designer . . . . Andrew Clancy
Costume Designer . . . . Migle Ryan
Lighting Designer . . . . Cillian O'Donnell
Sound Designer . . . . Sean Sweeney
Production Stage Manager . . . . Nicholas Sturman
Assistant Stage Manager . . . . Jack Hughes
Social Media & PR Manager . . . . Beth Strahan
Media Content Manager . . . . Kate Devaney
Poster & Cover Design . . . . Burcu Yılmaz

Glass Mask Theatre is an intimate boutique theatre situated in the heart of Dublin city where every seat is a front row seat. Under the artistic direction of Rex Ryan, it stages exciting new Irish and international plays accompanied by a top quality food and drink service.

Who the hell knows who we are, but the mission of the company is to stage all new Irish and international work, in our strikingly immersive Dublin venue, with a bunch of wild committed theatre artists. We want to uplift the souls of the people who join us and make a theatre ritual every night for our audience.

Founded in 2018 by Rex and Migle Ryan, the company is composed of a bunch of like-minded pirate souls of Irish Theatre who have been gifted with a spectacular venue in Dublin City Centre to stage all NEW plays with a full ritual of food and drink pre-show as part of the experience.

We were named theatre company of the year in our first year active with nothing but a can of tuna and the dreams of a band of stoic theatre artists to our name. Today, Glass Mask is the top new writing theatre in Dublin. We produce all new Irish plays alongside international premieres from some of the best playwrights in the world.

From our immersive Dawson Street Venue, we attempt to connect people from all walks of life with visceral, raw and joyous theatre. We have seen the power of this small temple over the last few years grow and grow. We have had the most life-affirming and uplifting experiences making and sharing work that we think speaks to the hearts of the humans who walk through the doors of the place.

Join us.

Take a risk on a new play.

Step out of comfort and confront the mayhem of life on a stage with a group of strangers.

We're trying to build a place for everyone.

That means YOU.

THANK YOU

Carla Kelly, Denis Coffey, Catherine Coffey, Denise Coffey, Johnny Martin, Kim Coffey, Niall O'Sullivan, Rex Ryan, Migle Ryan, Miriam Boyle, Vincent Boyle, Noel Kelly, Claire Kelly, Emma Kelly, Imelda Brophy, Maria Brophy, Luke Griffin, Peter Gaynor, Amanda Farley. My brilliant agents Holly Carey and Iain Mullins. Oli Gordon and the wonderful people at Samuel French. And the brilliant cast and crew for bringing this play to life.

CAST

ALAN DEVINE | Older

Alan can currently be seen in the role of Ealdorman of Kent in the Netflix series *Valhalla*. He was recently seen in the role of Donald MacIntosh in the creative documentary *Prisoners of the Moon*, directed by Johnny Gogan. He is one of Irish Television's most recognizable faces, having played Louie Gleeson on RTÉ's most popular series *Fair City*.

Television credits include: BBC's acclaimed series *The Tudors*, directed by Charles McDougal; *Trouble In Paradise*, directed by Eimer Reynolds; *Custer's Last Stand Up*, directed by Dearbhla Walsh for BBC/RTÉ; *Nighthawks (Sketches)*, directed by David McKenna, and *Glenroe*, both for RTÉ.

Film credits include: *The Gift*, directed by Damian O' Callaghan; *Black Ice*, directed by Johnny Gorgan; *Ghostwood*, directed by Justin O'Brien; *King Arthur*, directed by Antoine Fuqua, and *Veronica Guerin*, in which he played the role of Gerry Hutch, and was directed under Joel Schumacher.

Some of Alan's vast theatre work includes: *Macbeth* with Siren Productions; *Romeo and Juliet* with Kabosh Theatre Company; *Hard Times* with Storytellers Theatre; *Hamlet* with Second Age Theatre in which he played the leading role and *The Tempest* with Da Vinci theatre.

CRAIG CONNOLLY | Younger

Craig graduated from the Lir Academy of Dramatic Arts, Trinity College Dublin, with a BA in Acting in 2015. Recent credits include a recurring role in RTÉ's *Fair City* and a four-year run in the multi-award-winning West End production of *Harry Potter & The Cursed Child* (Sonia Friedman).

Craig's theatre credits include appearances at The Abbey Theatre with roles in *Jimmy's Hall* (2017, dir. Graham McLaren) and John Tiffany's *Let The Right One In* (2017); also numerous collaborations with the multi-award-winning ANU Productions, credits including *These Rooms*, *Sunder* and *On Corporation Street* in collaboration with Home Theatre company in Manchester (dir. Louise Lowe).

Prior to his professional training at The Lir; Craig worked as a young performer with companies such as Druid (*The Silver Tassie*, 2010, dir. Garry Hynes) and Long Road Productions (*I, Keano*, National Tour, 2008).

Screen credits include: *Misread* (2023, Ardan/RTÉ), *The Cabin* (2011, Hallmark TV), *The Hideaways* (2010, dir. Agnès Merlet) and *Roy* (2009, BBC/RTÉ).

Craig is also an accomplished musician, singing and playing piano, guitar, drums and ukulele. He is trained in ballet, tap and contemporary dance and has worked with award-winning movement directors Dermot Bolger (Cois Céim) and Steven Hoggett (Frantic Assembly).

CREATIVE

LEE COFFEY | Writer

Lee is a writer based in Dublin. He is a founding member and Creative Director of contemporary theatre company Bitter Like A Lemon. He was one of six writers selected for the 2018 New Playwrights Programme to mark the Lyric Theatre Belfast's 50th year celebrations. He was a participant in Six In The Attic in 2018–2019, an Irish Theatre Institute initiative for emerging talent. He was also a participant in the prestigious Rough Magic SEEDS programme in 2016–2017.

Lee's plays include the critically acclaimed *G.O.D.* (Dublin Theatre Festival), *In Our Veins* (Abbey Theatre), *Leper + Chip* (Theatre Upstairs; Project Arts Centre; Edinburgh Fringe Festival; Electric Picnic; Lyric Theatre Belfast; axis:Ballymun, Cork; Inis Nua Theatre Company, Philadelphia, USA), Peruvian Voodoo (Theatre Upstairs), *Slice, The Thief* (Smock Alley, axis:Ballymun), *Murder of Crows* (Theatre Upstairs, Project Arts Centre, Garter Lane, Lyric Theatre Belfast), *From All Sides* (Dublin Fringe Festival), *The First Irish Coffee* (Laughter Lounge) and the radio play *The Matron* as a part of Dead Air (Bram Stoker Festival). In 2020 *Leper + Chip* and *Slice, The Thief* were adapted for film as a part of Dublin Port Company's The Pumphouse Presents alongside axis:Ballymun, ANU Productions and Fishamble. Lee is currently under commission from leading theatre companies in Ireland and Europe. Lee is published multiple times by Samuel French and productions of his published works are regularly performed by theatre companies worldwide.

IAN TONER | Director

As an actor, Ian's stage credits include *Punk Rock* (Lyric Theatre), *Look Back in Anger* (Gate Theatre), *Double Cross* (Lyric/Abbey co-production) and *Children of the Sun* (Rough Magic/Abbey Theatre). Notable screen credits include *Catch-22* (Hulu), *Redwater* (BBC) and *Klondike* (TG4).

His debut play *Animalia* won the BBC Radio Northern Ireland Award and the Fishamble Award for best new writing. It was nominated for the Stewart Parker award and the Bewley's Little Gem Award the same year. He has written several other plays and is a script writer for *Fair City*.

As a director, credits include *Her Da is Old* and *The Dole Wide World* (both Glass Mask Theatre).

REX RYAN | Creative Director

Rex Ryan is the artistic director of Glass Mask Theatre Company. He is a writer, actor and director.

MIGLE RYAN | Creative Producer/Costume Designer

Migle Ryan is the creative producer at Glass Mask Theatre Company.

Rex and Migle have produced over thirty new Irish plays and have brought new Irish work around the world to audiences and critical acclaim.

ANDREW CLANCY | Set Designer

Andrew Clancy is a sculptor and set designer. His work is in both public and private collections. In terms of set design, he initially designed for Pan Pan Theatre, almost accidentally really, as they were operating outside the usual set design box and needed something new. Starting with *Deflowerfucked*, mid-nineties, through *Oedipus Loves You*, *Macbeth 7*, *One – Healing With Theatre*, *The Idiots*, and finally *Embers* (2014). Tangentially to this he was asked to design children's shows. Probably because his designs were more artistic than architectural.

Anyway, lots of shows for Barnstorm, from *Jack*, right through all the shows till now. Various other children's shows around the country. *Patient Gloria* for Gina Moxley and *In Vena Cava* for Ella Clarke in 2018. *A Very Old Man With Enormous Wings* and *Lost Lear* for Dan Colley and most recently *The Lottery*. And a number for Dead Centre: *Souvenir*, *Lippy*, *Chekhov's First Play*, *Hamnet*, *Beckett's Room* and *To Be A Machine*. Brú Theatre: *Not a Word* and *Somnium*. Glass Mask: *Men's Business* and *Jigsaw*.

Lots of other shows and multiple puppets, masks and sculptural props over the years for most of the Irish theatre companies. All in the same Canon really. Ranging from the slightly unusual to the utterly so.

CILLIAN O'DONNELL | Lighting Designer

Cillian is a Dublin-based lighting designer and theatre maker. He has previously worked with Glass Mask as lighting designer for *The Dole Wide World*. Cillian is a co-founder of the new theatre company Fungus & Moss, with whom he wrote and produced *TOO BIG TO TRY* for the Scene + Heard Festival, and the upcoming North Devon Theatrefest. Cillian has designed for numerous theatre productions, including Dublin Fringe, Edinburgh Fringe, and shows in The Samuel Beckett, Smock Alley, and Pavillion Theatre.

SEAN SWEENEY | Sound Designer

Sean is a Dublin-based sound engineer and music producer with a strong foundation in contemporary performance and audio production. After studying at Sound Training College, where he specialized in audio production and project management, Sean has built a diverse portfolio spanning studio work, live sound, and theatre.

He has collaborated with a wide range of artists including Bold Love, Skinner, Basht, Oceanna, and Lavery, contributing his technical expertise and creative touch to their recordings and performances. Sean also ventured into sound design for theatre, working with Rex Ryan on the play *Road to Joe*, where he was responsible for crafting the show's immersive audio landscape.

In addition to his work in music and theatre, Sean led a full D&B audio system installation at the Briary Gap Theatre, overseeing both the setup and fine-tuning of the system to ensure optimal performance.

NICHOLAS STURMAN | Production Stage Manager

Nick is a Dublin-based director and stage manager, currently working as company manager for Glass Mask Theatre. With a Theatre Arts Degree from Clark University in Worcester, Massachusetts, he has worked as a stage manager and assistant director for several Glass Mask Theatre productions. He has also been an operator and venue liaison for both the Dublin Theatre Festival and the Dublin Gay Theatre festival. He has also worked on several independent theatre projects in various roles, both on and backstage.

JACK HUGHES | Assistant Stage Manager

Jack is a Dublin-based playwright. He has worked on several amateur productions in the capacity of stage management, producing, writing and directing.

BETH STRAHAN | Social Media & PR Manager

Beth is a Dublin-based director and producer from Belfast. She is the current PR Manager for Glass Mask Theatre and Co-Producer of ABLAZE Productions. Directing credits include *Cailíní* (Lyric Theatre, ABLAZE Pros, May 2024), *Five Year Stand* (Grand Opera House, Brunswick Productions, July 2024) and *Double Down* (Droichead Arts Centre, ABLAZE Pros, March 2025).

KATE DEVANEY | Media Content Manager

Kate is currently the Media Content Manager for Glass Mask Theatre. She is also a writer and has an MA in Writing for Stage and Screen from University College Dublin. Her work has been staged at Scene + Heard, The Makers Ensemble and workshopped at New Perspectives Theatre, New York. She is currently working on her first novel.

BURCU YILMAZ | Poster & Cover Design

Burcu Yılmaz is a visual artist and illustrator from Turkey, currently based in Dublin. She studied Ceramics in high school and holds a degree in Visual Communication Design. With a background in art direction, she worked for seven years as an assistant art director in film and theatre, gaining valuable experience from inspiring creative teams. Burcu has been illustrating digitally for the past three years. Her work is often influenced by light and warmth – the sun is her biggest source of inspiration, energising and bringing colour to everything she creates.

CHARACTERS

JIM (OLDER) – 2025
JIM (YOUNGER) – 2005

SETTING & TIME

Dublin, 2005 and 2025.

AUTHOR'S NOTE

In Part One, actor one plays **JIM (OLDER)**, actor two plays all other characters **(YOUNGER)**.

In Part Two, actor two plays **JIM (YOUNGER)**, actor one plays all other characters **(OLDER)**.

For Carla. A chuisle, mo chroí.

(A black space. Lights pulse during the following. The intro of "Now That You're Gone" by The Raconteurs plays on a loop as the lights pulse.)

(As the lights and sound build to a climax, we see two figures in the darkness. The following dialogue builds with the lights and sound.)

OLDER. Get up.

YOUNGER. Get up.

OLDER. Get up.

YOUNGER. Get up.

OLDER. Get up.

YOUNGER. Get the fuck up!

      (Snap. Lights up. 2025.)

OLDER. What?

YOUNGER. I said, get the fuck up.

OLDER. I open my eyes.

    There stands the cunt.

    I say cunt.

    But I'm asleep and blocking.

    Blocking the door to his job.

YOUNGER. I need to get to fucking work, man.

OLDER. I stand up, slowly and unsteadily.

    Pack up my stuff.

YOUNGER. Come on, fuck's sake.

OLDER. Give me a sec.

Ever been to a festival?

This shit takes time.

He backs off.

A few steps.

I'm packed.

He warily moves around me.

As I move aside.

He forces himself to the door.

A shoe shop.

Good on you, man.

Changing the fucking world, you are.

YOUNGER. At least I'm doing something with myself.

The fuck do you do?

Poxy waster.

OLDER. Hope you get an aul' miserable fuck with bunions you could hike up.

YOUNGER. Sooner the better, they clear the streets of you leeches.

            (Slight pause.)

OLDER. He goes, I go.

Wanker.

Cleary's clock says nine.

It's warm, coming into summer.

Thankfully.

Winters are hard.

Spring and summer is like the start of a relationship.

Warm, everything's bright and full of hope.

Winter, is when you're married forty years and you think, if I've to look at this fucking face one more time.

Tourists and tour groups already out and about.

YOUNGER. On your left you'll see The Spire.

OLDER. Waste of money.

YOUNGER. And over here we have the GPO.

OLDER. I pass the masses.

I've a few hours before I try see her.

Street dealers out already.

YOUNGER. Get your oranges!

OLDER. Howya, Angela

YOUNGER. Ah, Jim. How are ya?

OLDER. Keeping on.

YOUNGER. That's all you can do.

Here.

OLDER. A couple of apples and a banana.

YOUNGER. Want an avocado too?

OLDER. Jaysus, you lot have changed.

YOUNGER. You have to have what the punters want.

OLDER. True.

YOUNGER. All those posh hipsters love the avo.

OLDER. You'll be doing flat whites next.

YOUNGER. I'll flatten you next.

OLDER. See ya, Angela.

YOUNGER. Be good.

OLDER. Cunt's ninety and still on her stall.

Proper aul Dub.

Wind worn and hard as nails.

You have to be. I hear her talking about me as I leave.

YOUNGER. Poor fella. Alone. His whole family/

OLDER. Liffey Street, across the Liffey and onto the quays.

I usually head for breakfast in Vincent DePaul on Eustace Street.

YOUNGER. Let me fucking in, you pox.

OLDER. Sexy fella outside a shop.

YOUNGER. I just need to use the machine.

OLDER. Bag of bottles.

YOUNGER. Come on, I'll be quick.

OLDER. Worker not having it.

YOUNGER. You called me a prick last time you were in.

OLDER. I try pass.

YOUNGER. Ya are a prick. And if you don't let me in, you're only proving me point.

OLDER. He tries to push by and he's stopped. He grabs the worker.

YOUNGER. Now, you're makin' me assault ya: only want to recycle. For the planet, yeah?

OLDER. Not having it. They reef out of each other and stumble into the shop.

YOUNGER. Me good top.

OLDER. I watch them.

From the door.

Punchin' lumps out of each other.

The man's detained.

YOUNGER. Get off me.

This is Gucci, Bro.

OLDER. I look down.

His bottles left on the path.

YOUNGER. Here, you, you aul fuck.

Don't touch them.

OLDER. I pick them up.

YOUNGER. Here!

OLDER. And walk into him.

YOUNGER. Ah, sound, Pal.

OLDER. Thanks for these.

Couldn't have out run you.

YOUNGER. Prick.

OLDER. He's reefed out back.

And off I walk.

Bottles in hand.

I walk. Dublin talks.

YOUNGER. S'cuse me, guys.

OLDER. All strands.

YOUNGER. Get outta' me fucking way.

OLDER. Blendin'.

YOUNGER. Oh my God, I asked for oat milk in my flat white.

OLDER. I head down the side of the Olympia.

    Stash my things.

    Quiet.

    I let the air fill the lungs.

    In. Out.

        (Slight pause.)

    A family pass me.

    Husband, wife, daughter.

        (Slight pause.)

    Memories intrude.

        (Snap.)

YOUNGER. Can't believe you did that.

OLDER. I didn't.

YOUNGER. Get out.

OLDER. Listen to me.

YOUNGER. Get the fuck out now.

OLDER. Please.

YOUNGER. We never want to see you again.

OLDER. Just give me a chance to/

        (Snap.)

YOUNGER. Where the fuck did you get them?

OLDER. Snapped out of it. Ger.

YOUNGER. On the swipe again, Jimbo?

OLDER. Opportunities, Ger.

    Have to take them.

YOUNGER. Good haul. How long did that take you?

OLDER. About five mins.

YOUNGER. I see. You won't always be able to outrun them.

OLDER. I didn't have to today.

All that counts.

Just today.

YOUNGER. Haven't seen you 'round lately.

OLDER. Trying to keep the head down.

YOUNGER. Any chance you'd throw us a euro or two out of that?

OLDER. Not sure about that, Ger.

YOUNGER. Ah, come on. How long have we known each other?

OLDER. Too long.

YOUNGER. Just a couple of euro.

OLDER. Just a couple of euro.

YOUNGER. That's all I need.

OLDER. Fine. You'll be here?

YOUNGER. Amn't I always?

OLDER. Ger the manipulator.

YOUNGER. You're too good to me, spoil me, you do/

OLDER. You're getting your money so give over.

I'll be back in a bit.

I'm leaving me stuff here, don't knick it.

YOUNGER. I'm grand.

A mouldy sleeping bag and a three-year-old's tent.

OLDER. You'll never let me live that down, will ya?

YOUNGER. You swiped a kid's tent, lad.

OLDER. She was a little bollocks.

YOUNGER. Yeah, yeah.

OLDER. Off I go.

Bottle bank in Lidl, George's St.

There are two, so no fuckers behind you waiting.

Is it a poxy money racket? Yes.

But is it good for people like me? Too right.

I bet you see us. Routing.

In the bins.

Grabbing the bottles.

Gobblin' them up.

Good for the planet.

Good for our pockets.

A few hours, few bottles.

And you're laughin'.

Well, given, I stroked these.

But the logic is still sound.

I'm there. Load them all.

Fifteen euro.

Thanks, Sexy.

A really good haul.

I queue for the refund.

Wait.

And a couple of people in front of me.

(Slight pause.)

Is that her?

YOUNGER. Next, please.

OLDER. Is it. Chloe?

YOUNGER. Have you Lidl plus?

OLDER. Yes, it's her.

YOUNGER. Next, please.

OLDER. She moves off.

YOUNGER. Sir?

OLDER. I watch her leave.

YOUNGER. Sir?

OLDER. Chloe.

YOUNGER. Are you fucking listening to me, sir?

OLDER. Sorry. Yes.

Did you just swear?

YOUNGER. It's been a morning, sir.

OLDER. That it has.

Refund. Gone.

I rush out.

Look left, look right.

Can't spot her.

Then I see her.

Heading towards the green.

I follow her.

Hanging back.

She's with a couple of friends and then heads into the park.

And parks on the grass.

I take a bench across.

A bit away.

I do this every day.

Well, I try.

To see her.

I know she works around town.

So I get up.

Get food.

And hope to see her.

Just to see her face.

I sit there.

And I just watch.

Her smile.

Her laugh.

Glowing in the sun.

I wish I was sitting there with her.

I wish I could even say hello to her.

After what feels like a minute.

Her friends leave.

She's alone.

Will I go over?

No, we never go over.

I think back to when she was born.

    (Snap.)

I'm handed this little ball of mush.

Holy fuck.

I wept. Instantly.

She was just...perfect.

YOUNGER. Do we have a name?

OLDER. We do.

Chloe.

Hey, lil' nugget.

I'm your Da.

(*Snap.*)

I'm snapped out of it as she packs up.

And before I know it.

I'm moving.

Walking.

My legs taking me there.

What are youse at, you mad cunts.

And they stop, just beside her.

Hi, darling.

(*Pause.*)

YOUNGER. You... Jesus, you look like shit.

OLDER. You look/

YOUNGER. Don't/

OLDER. Beautiful/

YOUNGER. I've to go.

OLDER. Please, just one conversation.

YOUNGER. Why would I want to talk to you?

OLDER. Because I'm your Da.

YOUNGER. Still clinging to that title?

OLDER. You sound like/

YOUNGER. Me Ma? Nan?

OLDER. Both of them.

YOUNGER. Well, when you're raised by someone, you tend to pick up a few things.

OLDER. How's/

YOUNGER. Ma?

OLDER. No.

YOUNGER. Not want to know how she is?

OLDER. Why would I?

YOUNGER. Unbelievable.

OLDER. My life was ruined.

YOUNGER. You did that yourself.

OLDER. Love/

YOUNGER. I was told.

The screaming.

All the shouting.

All that shit you were on.

OLDER. I'm sober.

YOUNGER. Sure you are.

OLDER. Really, I am.

Ten years.

(Slight pause.)

It was always that shit.

Making situations worse.

YOUNGER. It was you.

You and your temper.

OLDER. Stop.

YOUNGER. She's happy now anyway.

OLDER. How's your Nan?

> *(Slight pause.)*

YOUNGER. I've to go.

OLDER. How is she? Eighty-five now.

Silence.

As she walks off.

Tell her I'm okay.

I sit.

Where she sat.

In the sun.

As she did.

After a second the sun is blocked out.

Chloe.

YOUNGER. Nan isn't well.

OLDER. What?

YOUNGER. She's in Harold's Cross.

OLDER. The hospice?

YOUNGER. That's all I'm telling you.

Now leave me alone.

OLDER. Please, Chloe.

What ward, what room?

YOUNGER. I'm not telling you.

OLDER. She goes off.

The sun falls on me again.

I watch her until she disappears from view.

The hospice?

The fucking hospice?

I don't know how long I sat there.

But it was long enough that the ranger came.

YOUNGER. Here, c'mon, we're closing.

OLDER. Grand.

YOUNGER. Now, out the fucking gate.

I know what you dirty cunts do in the bushes.

Like rabbits.

OLDER. I walk. Aimless. Hapless.

The hospice?

Soon, I'm back in the lane.

YOUNGER. You took your time.

OLDER. Not now, Ger.

YOUNGER. Face like a slapped arse.

Not as much as you thought?

OLDER. Here's your three euro.

YOUNGER. Hungry cunt.

OLDER. Ger, shut the fuck up.

YOUNGER. Who pissed in your cornflakes?

OLDER. Me Ma's in the hospice. Up in Harold's cross.

YOUNGER. Ah, youngfella. I'm sorry. Cancer?

OLDER. I don't know.

YOUNGER. What you do you mean you don't know?

OLDER. I wasn't told.

YOUNGER. By who?

OLDER. Chloe.

YOUNGER. Your daughter?

OLDER. Yeah.

YOUNGER. Ah, you're still on the lookout for her.

OLDER. Every day.

(Pause.)

YOUNGER. So when are you going to see her?

OLDER. You high?

YOUNGER. I fucking wish.

OLDER. I can't go and see her.

YOUNGER. Why not?

OLDER. Because I haven't spoken to her in years.

Not since it all happened.

YOUNGER. That's a long time, lad.

And trust me.

If she hasn't long left.

I bet she'd welcome a visit from her son.

OLDER. I couldn't.

YOUNGER. Why? How much fucking worse can it get, Jimbo?

OLDER. Not much.

YOUNGER. Not fucking much.

(Slight pause.)

OLDER. Well, I'll see you, Ger.

YOUNGER. See ya, Jim. And go, or you'll regret it.

OLDER. I leave. An' walk.

　　Until the sun's left us.

　　I know Ger's right but...

　　How can I?

　　I haven't seen her in twenty years.

　　I think about her every day.

　　Her and Chloe.

　　She's my Ma.

　　We were a team.

　　When that cunt of a da was still around.

　　But...

　　She thinks I betrayed her.

　　　　(Snap.)

YOUNGER. Never become like your father.

OLDER. I won't.

YOUNGER. Promise me.

OLDER. I promise.

YOUNGER. I believe you.

　　　　(Snap.)

OLDER. I usually stay in town.

　　I've a couple of spots.

　　But tonight.

　　I walk towards the canal.

Only one thing on my mind.

Me Ma.

Harold's Cross.

The hospice.

It's just across the bridge.

So I'll camp here tonight.

And see what tomorrow brings.

Maybe I'll see her.

Maybe I won't.

YOUNGER. Yeow, go on, you dog, ya!

OLDER. It's the summer.

YOUNGER. Neck it, neck it.

OLDER. So the canal attracts.

YOUNGER. Bleeding lightweight, bro.

OLDER. Hordes.

Hordes of hipsters.

Drinking IPA.

Devil's Dick.

Banshee's Hole.

All with the ridiculous.

I sit on a bench and watch them all.

Mullets, moustaches and not a sock between them.

The lads dressed like girls.

The girls dressed like lads.

Music blares.

Shite.

It's no "Summer Lovin."

I move to a quieter spot.

Down, near the underpass.

A bench.

I sprawl out.

Settling in.

Probably kip here.

YOUNGER. No.

OLDER. For a few hours.

YOUNGER. Stop.

OLDER. See how I get on.

YOUNGER. I said, stop.

OLDER. I sit up and there's a couple.

YOUNGER. Come on.

OLDER. Messing around.

YOUNGER. You said you wanted some privacy.

OLDER. He seems a little eager.

YOUNGER. Don't be a little virgin.

OLDER. Just stop, youngfella.

YOUNGER. I've changed my mind.

OLDER. Walk away.

YOUNGER. Well, I haven't.

OLDER. Fuck this.

YOUNGER. I told you/

OLDER. She said no, you little prick.

YOUNGER. Let go of him.

OLDER. We're not going far.

YOUNGER. Mister, it's okay. Let him go.

OLDER. Don't worry, I am.

YOUNGER. Wait, don't/

OLDER. I skull haul the little fucker into the canal.

He doesn't like that.

YOUNGER. Help, help.

I can't swim.

OLDER. Are you okay?

YOUNGER. I'm okay.

OLDER. Don't let anyone touch you like that.

YOUNGER. I won't.

OLDER. His no sock cronies use a stick and pull him out.

YOUNGER. Oh my God, Tadgh, you could've drowned.

OLDER. Go home now, love.

YOUNGER. Thank you.

OLDER. I leave and park on a bench further down the canal.

And rest.

(*Slight pause.*)

YOUNGER. Mind if I join you?

OLDER. Chloe. I wouldn't mind at all.

She sits beside me.

And we don't speak.

For a little bit.

So much I want to ask.

But I don't.

We just sit.

And it's bliss.

Then...

YOUNGER. I saw what happened. I'm on my way back from seeing Nan.

      (Slight pause.)

OLDER. It was nothing.

YOUNGER. Your man sounded like a prick.

OLDER. Good thing he was wearing second hand clothes.

We smile.

      (Slight pause.)

YOUNGER. I think ten years.

Is pretty amazing.

OLDER. Thank you.

YOUNGER. You should be proud.

OLDER. I am.

YOUNGER. I am too.

OLDER. Chloe, you know that I/

YOUNGER. Don't. Let's leave it where it is.

We can't get that time back.

OLDER. No, we can't.

      (Slight pause.)

You know when I wake up, what my purpose is?

To see you.

YOUNGER. To see me?

OLDER. Ten years ago, I saw you.

For the first time since your christening.

You were a kid, walking with your Mam.

Just seeing you.

How you'd grown.

It made me happy.

And I can't explain it.

I've been sober ever since.

I didn't want to score.

I didn't want a hit.

I just wanted to see you again.

So, with my life, I figured, that was a good purpose to have.

I made it my daily goal.

Trying to see you.

Most I wouldn't.

Some, I would.

And today, I did.

And spoke to you.

One for the books.

> *(Slight pause.)*

YOUNGER. Today, did you not guess how I knew it was you?

OLDER. Actually, no.

YOUNGER. Nan has pictures. Lots of pictures.

OLDER. You looked at them?

YOUNGER. All of them.

Asking...why, you know?

OLDER. I'd do the same.

YOUNGER. How's your Mam?

(Slight pause.)

I better go.

But look after yourself.

OLDER. You too.

YOUNGER. I'll keep an eye for you too.

OLDER. I'd like that.

(Slight pause.)

YOUNGER. Nan is in room six.

OLDER. What?

YOUNGER. You being up this way.

Her just up the road.

I assume you're thinking of going.

And I think you should.

(Slight pause.)

Go first thing.

Mam won't be there.

She'll be working.

And she's in Potter's Ward.

Room six.

OLDER. I will, thanks.

YOUNGER. See you around.

OLDER. I hope so, Nugget.

    And off she goes.

       (Slight pause.)

    The next morning.

    I wake.

    With half a bench up my arse.

    Not the best sleep.

    I can't wait around.

    Need to get there.

    Before that fuck arrives.

    I need something first.

    An old friend is nearby.

    I stash my things.

    I stroll over.

    Feeling rough.

    Like I was the one in the canal.

    I approach the reception.

YOUNGER. Eh, can I help you?

OLDER. Yes, I'd like to speak to Steo, please.

YOUNGER. There's nobody here by that name.

OLDER. He owns the place.

    He's a friend of mine.

    Can you tell him Jim Shaw is here?

YOUNGER. Sir, there's nobody by/

OLDER. Listen, I'm not leaving until you get him.

YOUNGER. One second.

OLDER. I sit and wait.

YOUNGER. Sir, there's a man. A scruffy man here.

OLDER. We're friends.

YOUNGER. He says you're friends.

OLDER. Old friends.

YOUNGER. Old friends.

OLDER. BFF's/

YOUNGER. He'll be minute.

OLDER. Thanks.

> *(Slight pause.)*

YOUNGER. Jesus Christ. Look at this fella.

OLDER. Steo. Good to see you.

YOUNGER. Fuck, man. I thought you were dead.

OLDER. Keeping on.

YOUNGER. Come in, come in.

OLDER. We head to his office.

YOUNGER. Holy shit.

Jim Shaw, in my office.

OLDER. You're doing well, Steo.

YOUNGER. Second biggest gym chain in the county.

OLDER. Delighted for you.

YOUNGER. Just need Flyefit to fuck off.

> *(Slight pause.)*

Jim Bleedin' Shaw. What the fuck happened, man?

OLDER. With what?

YOUNGER. Everything.

You, the family, I heard some crazy stories.

OLDER. It just all blew up.

YOUNGER. I know you both used to fight.

After you'd go on the session.

But for it to get to that?

OLDER. It just got too much.

And it erupted.

YOUNGER. At the Christening.

OLDER. Yeah.

YOUNGER. I was there but I was off my face.

OLDER. Everyone was.

YOUNGER. Just remember you both.

The blood.

OLDER. That's what everyone remembers.

YOUNGER. Was that all her blood?

OLDER. Yeah.

YOUNGER. I tried to reach out after.

To see what the story was.

OLDER. I vanished.

Fell in to a hole.

Lost it all.

YOUNGER. Legal fees aren't cheap.

OLDER. No, an' fuck all use it did.

YOUNGER. Suspended sentence, yeah?

OLDER. Served a year.

An' when I came out.

No job, no house, no family, nothin'.

Branded a monster.

Drank an' snorted whatever money I had.

Gradually going downhill.

Until I ended up...here.

YOUNGER. I'm sorry, Jim.

OLDER. Everyone turned against me.

YOUNGER. And can I ask/

OLDER. Did I do it?

YOUNGER. Yeah.

OLDER. We'd get messy, both of us.

It was that long ago now.

Who knows what actually happened?

YOUNGER. Okay, man. It is great to see you, but/

OLDER. What do I want?

YOUNGER. What do you fucking want?

OLDER. A shower.

YOUNGER. A shower?

OLDER. Yeah. I'm going to see my Ma today.

And I want to be clean.

Presentable.

YOUNGER. Say no more.

How is she?

OLDER. Good. Yeah, she's, good.

YOUNGER. It's good you two made up.

OLDER. Yeah.

YOUNGER. I've a private shower back here.

And put these on after.

OLDER. A fucking tracksuit?

YOUNGER. A clean tracksuit.

That's usually eighty euro with a monthly membership attached.

OLDER. Robbing them blind.

YOUNGER. Second biggest in the county.

I'll pop back in a little bit.

> *(Slight pause.)*

OLDER. I shower.

And I can't describe it.

Things you take for granted.

Hot water.

Soap.

It's been a while since my last.

I rub and scrub every inch of me.

You could eat your dinner off me.

Sorry about that visual.

YOUNGER. Here, you still in there?

OLDER. Just done.

YOUNGER. Good thing water charges didn't come in.

OLDER. Out. Dry. Dressed.

Steo. Thanks, man.

YOUNGER. No problem.

You should have come to me.

I could have helped you.

OLDER. I guess I figured you'd hate me too.

YOUNGER. I've always hated you.

You've always been a prick.

OLDER. Thanks, man.

YOUNGER. Don't be a stranger.

There's always a shower here.

OLDER. Might take you up on that.

YOUNGER. I'll see you soon.

OLDER. I wave to the receptionist as I leave.

And head for Harold's Cross.

Half way there.

I feel something.

In me pocket.

An envelope.

I open it.

Three hundred euro.

YOUNGER. Here's that money I owed you.

Keep on keepin' on. Steo.

OLDER. I can hear my heart beating.

Harder with each step and I'm not even there yet.

I enter the gates.

Get to reception.

YOUNGER. Good morning, can I help you?

OLDER. I'm here to see my mother. Angie Shaw.

YOUNGER. I didn't know she had a son.

OLDER. Her best kept secret.

YOUNGER. She's in Potter's, room six.

OLDER. Yes. Thank you.

I walk down the hall.

To her room.

Get to it.

Take a deep breath.

And another.

You can do this, Jim.

What's the worst that can happen?

I enter.

Pushing the door open.

And there she is.

My Ma.

She looks so small in that big bed.

I just see a tuft of grey hair.

Popping out from the top.

I approach.

And sit beside her.

After a few minutes.

She stirs.

And slowly sits up.

My heart goes into overdrive.

Feeling like my chest is about to burst.

She's so small.

So frail.

Like she's wasted away.

She takes in the room.

And lands on me.

YOUNGER. How strong is that medication?

OLDER. Howya, Ma.

YOUNGER. James. Is that you?

OLDER. It's me, Ma.

YOUNGER. Why are you in a tracksuit?

> *(Jim smiles.)*

You look like a six year old.

OLDER. It's great to see you, Ma.

YOUNGER. It's good to see you too, Son.

> *(Slight pause.)*

How long has it been?

OLDER. Twenty years, give or take.

YOUNGER. God, that long. And how did you know/

OLDER. That you were here? I ran into Chloe.

YOUNGER. She spoke to you?

OLDER. I helped her with a...situation.

YOUNGER. You were always good in...situations.

> *(Slight pause.)*

OLDER. What happened, Ma?

YOUNGER. They found a lump.

OLDER. And have they given a time or/

YOUNGER. Son, I'm in a hospice.

It's a matter of days.

OLDER. Ma, I/

YOUNGER. Don't.

I've lived a good life.

OLDER. I'm sorry, for everything.

YOUNGER. Don't be. It's who you are.

The one good thing your father did.

Was give me you.

Then the one good thing you did.

Was give me her.

OLDER. She's beautiful.

YOUNGER. And with a heart of gold.

She's nothing like you.

OLDER. I'm not a bad/

YOUNGER. Son, listen.

It's gone. It's happened.

OLDER. Ma/

YOUNGER. You let love consume you.

God, remember how obsessed with Hayley you were?

OLDER. I loved her/

YOUNGER. Too much.

After it happened, you kept coming 'round.

Shouting and screaming.

Off your mind on that stuff.

OLDER. I'm sober a long time, Ma.

YOUNGER. Good. I'm happy for you.

But it doesn't change what you became.

OLDER. I'm nothing like him.

YOUNGER. I've no more energy to lie.

OLDER. I'm not, I got rid of him.

Threw him out on the street.

YOUNGER. You did and I'll forever be grateful for that.

OLDER. It was you and me.

You and me.

Why didn't you help me?

YOUNGSTER. Help you?

OLDER. Yeah/

YOUNGSTER. Because I saw it.

Saw your rage.

That night I was watching Chloe.

An' when I got to the station.

You were exactly like your father.

In that little room. Roaring.

Talking to yourself.

Covered in blood.

I felt like I'd gone back in time.

OLDER. I'm not him.

YOUNGER. You are.

OLDER. I'm not.

YOUNGER. I think you should leave.

OLDER. Nothin' like him.

YOUNGER. Son/

OLDER. Nothin'!

> *(Slight pause.)*

YOUNGER. In thirty seconds.

If you're not gone.

I'm calling the nurse.

> *(Slight pause.)*

OLDER. Okay, I'll leave.

I'm sorry, Ma.

For everything.

YOUNGER. I am too.

OLDER. I love you.

YOUNGER. I love you too.

OLDER. I go to leave and/

> *(Slight pause.)*

The door opens.

> *(Slight pause.)*

Hayley.

YOUNGER. Jim.

OLDER. She stands there.

Still beautiful.

Even with the scars.

Coming to see my Ma.

My dyin' Ma.

While I'm hangin' together.

In a fucking tracksuit.

Donated by a former coke head.

This isn't fair.

This wasn't supposed to be my life.

This is her fault.

All her fault.

(*Slight pause.*)

I feel my brain start to move.

The anger moving it.

Shapin' it.

Shiftin' the pieces around.

A voice.

I haven't heard in years.

Pipes ups.

Speaks up.

YOUNGER. Look at this cow.

OLDER. What?

YOUNGER. It's been a while.

OLDER. No, no.

Leave me alone.

YOUNGER. Look what she's done to you.

OLDER. Stop.

YOUNGER. Look where you are.

OLDER. Stop.

YOUNGER. This isn't right.

Do you think it is?

OLDER. No.

YOUNGER. Exactly.

OLDER. There's this rage when I see her.

YOUNGER. Good, let it out.

OLDER. I can't.

YOUNGER. Your Ma is dying in that bed.

    And you can't stay.

    Why?

    Because of her.

OLDER. Yeah.

      (Slight pause.)

YOUNGER. I'm getting security.

OLDER. You don't have to do that, Hayley.

    Ma, why's she getting security?

YOUNGER. Because she's terrified of you.

OLDER. There's no need.

      (Slight pause.)

YOUNGER. Son, can do one last thing for me?

OLDER. What, Ma?

YOUNGER. Leave. And don't come back.

OLDER. I want to fix this. I want to make it right.

YOUNGER. Sir, can you come with us?

OLDER. I look at my Ma. I look at Hayley.

    Why did you do this, Hayley?

YOUNGER. Sir, please.

OLDER. All of it.

YOUNGER. Now!

OLDER. Why?

YOUNGER. Outside.

OLDER. Get your hands off me.

YOUNGER. You're leaving.

OLDER. Please, that's my Ma.

YOUNGER. I don't care.

OLDER. That's my Ma.

She's dying.

She's fuckin' dying.

> *(Slight pause.)*

The guard and two others drag me from the building.

My Ma cryin' in the bed.

And Hayley. Just watchin' on.

> *(Slight pause.)*

They throw me out the gate.

I get to my feet.

Fuck!

YOUNGER. Leave now, or we call the guards.

OLDER. See her in there, she's the one you need to be throwin' out.

I walk back towards the canal.

And plant on a bench.

Fuck me.

I sit.

All day.

Trying to ignore him.

YOUNGER. She strikes again.

OLDER. Stop.

YOUNGER. Plays you for a sap, again!

OLDER. I said stop.

YOUNGER. I guess you'll always be her bitch.

OLDER. Stop it, stop it, stop it!

>   *(Pause.)*

Why? Why is it always me?

The rain starts.

Perfect.

I have to say.

A drink would go well right now.

And anythin' else too.

No.

Don't, Jim.

Bad idea, man.

I walk for food instead.

Burger, and back to the canal.

I look for Chloe.

No sign.

I sleep.

YOUNGER. You need to go back up.

OLDER. I do.

YOUNGER. She can't die thinkin' this.

OLDER. You're right.

YOUNGER. I'm always right, we know this.

OLDER. I rise and head.

  Up and back to the hospice.

  Different person on reception.

  Great.

  Hi, I'm here to see my mother.

  Potter's ward, room six.

YOUNGER. Mrs. Shaw.

OLDER. Yes, thank you.

YOUNGER. I'm so sorry, Sir.

OLDER. No, yesterday was a mis/

YOUNGER. She passed away this morning.

      (Slight pause.)

OLDER. What?

YOUNGER. In her sleep. She never woke up.

OLDER. No.

YOUNGER. Sir/

OLDER. No.

YOUNGER. I'm sorry.

OLDER. This has to be a mistake.

YOUNGER. It isn't, I'm sorry for your loss.

OLDER. I ran, in a blur, to her room.

  Push the door open.

  Ma, Ma.

  I run to her bed.

  Ma, please.

  Open your eyes.

(Slight pause.)

I look to the side.

Chloe and Hayley.

YOUNGER. You should go, Jim.

With all the stress you caused yesterday.

OLDER. I don't listen to her.

I just hold my Ma's hand and block her out.

YOUNGER. You need to leave.

OLDER. I ignore her.

YOUNGER. She wouldn't want you here.

OLDER. I ignore her.

YOUNGER. You broke her heart.

OLDER. Shut up.

You and your venom.

All of it.

I step to her.

Is this what you wanted?

You ruined my life.

Ruined it!

And for what?

Because I used to go out?

Because I wasn't a good husband?

No, I wasn't.

I was a terrible husband.

But I loved you.

It didn't have to be this way.

YOUNGER. It's always someone else's fault.

　　Isn't it, Jim?

OLDER. No!

　　Chloe comes to me.

YOUNGER. You need to leave.

OLDER. I don't move.

YOUNGER. Please, Jim.

OLDER. An' I go.

YOUNGER. Abuser.

OLDER. Memories intrude.

　　Her voice echoes in my mind.

　　I walk.

　　Not seeing anything.

　　Just walkin'.

　　Everything's a blur.

YOUNGER. You alright?

OLDER. No.

YOUNGER. I'm here for ya.

OLDER. No, no, I don't need you.

YOUNGER. You need me more than ever.

OLDER. My brain rings.

　　Like it's going to blow up.

　　I need to go.

　　I need to escape.

　　I turn and head for town.

YOUNGER. That's the spirit.

OLDER. Lane way, in off Grafton.

YOUNGER. Ah, golden.

OLDER. I stop at a black door.

An' knock.

YOUNGER. Holy fuck.

OLDER. Comes over the buzzer.

An' I'm in.

I climb the stairs.

I haven't in years.

That I used to climb weekly.

The door opens.

YOUNGER. Get in here and give me a hug.

OLDER. Howya, Larry.

YOUNGER. Come in, come in.

Sit down, sit down.

OLDER. I do an' the door closes behind me.

YOUNGER. Fuck me. I thought you were dead.

OLDER. Just keeping on.

YOUNGER. Last time I saw you.

That christening.

OLDER. Yeah. Listen, Larry.

I'm not here for a reunion.

YOUNGER. The fuckin' blood/

OLDER. Larry/

YOUNGER. What can I do you for?

OLDER. Three bags.

YOUNGER. Three hundred.

OLDER. There you go.

YOUNGER. Threw a few pills in there too.

For old time's sake.

OLDER. Good seeing you, Larry.

As I leave.

YOUNGER. It was awful what happened, man.

(Slight pause.)

Why'd you hit her?

OLDER. See ya', Larry.

(Slight pause.)

I don't even leave the building.

In the hall.

(Slight pause.)

YOUNGER. Welcome back.

I've missed you.

OLDER. And I'm flyin'.

YOUNGER. Roamin'.

OLDER. Driftin' through the streets.

YOUNGER. A few heads we knew.

OLDER. Dens, I used to frequent.

YOUNGER. Bliss.

OLDER. Blackened windows.

Blackened hearts.

YOUNGER. Dog days are back.

OLDER. I take it all.

YOUNGER. The bag/

OLDER. The pills/

YOUNGER. An'tin/

OLDER. I'll take it.

   An' I do.

> *(Snap. Slight pause.)*

   I fall into a hole.

   That hole I lived in.

   One I don't want to come out of.

   An' as I lay there.

YOUNGER. Jim/

OLDER. Hayley?

YOUNGER. You promised.

OLDER. We were so happy.

YOUNGER. We were. And I'll always remember us that way.

> *(Slight pause.)*

   Son.

OLDER. Ma?

YOUNGER. You promised me.

> *(Slight pause.)*

OLDER. How did this become my life?

YOUNGER. You can still make it better.

OLDER. How?

   You're gone.

YOUNGER. It doesn't matter if you win or lose.

>   *(Slight pause.)*

OLDER. It's what you do with your dancin' shoes.

>   *(Slight pause.)*

YOUNGER. I know you tried, Son.

OLDER. I did.

I tried to be a good man.

YOUNGER. Now come say goodbye.

>   *(Snap. A ringing sounds, like a grenade has just gone off.)*

OLDER. The funeral.

Here, you.

What day is it?

YOUNGER. I don't know, Christmas Day?

OLDER. Fuck.

I leave the den.

The sun glares at me.

It's Tuesday.

The funeral's today.

>   *(Slight pause.)*

I know I shouldn't go.

YOUNGER. Course you should, man.

OLDER. But I have to/

YOUNGER. Yeah, confront this cunt.

OLDER. No, I'm just stayin' in the shadows.

YOUNGER. Yeah, the shadows.

OLDER. I get to Francis Street church.

Just in time.

As the cortege passes.

I bless myself but lean my face away.

They park.

Exit the cars.

Hayley, Chloe.

They wheel my Ma inside.

An' everyone follows.

I pause.

(Slight pause.)

YOUNGER. No, no.

OLDER. I can't go in.

YOUNGER. Listen.

She fucked you over.

But she fucked me over too.

We're goin'/

OLDER. We enter the church.

YOUNGER. Good crowd.

OLDER. She was a popular woman.

YOUNGER. She was.

OLDER. I look at them up the front.

I should be there.

YOUNGER. I've known this family a long time.

Christened young Chloe.

It's an honour to be here today.

For Angie, a great woman.

An' now, ladies an' gentlemen.

We'll have Hayley, to say a few words.

    (Slight pause.)

OLDER. She's doin' the eulogy.

My mother's eulogy.

YOUNGER. It's great to see everyone here.

I know it would mean a great deal to Angie.

OLDER. I look at her.

Charm.

Beauty.

Grace.

Everyone eatin' out of her hand.

YOUNGER. Angie, didn't have many people.

Just me, and Chloe and/

OLDER. Fucking me!

YOUNGER. What are you doing, man?

OLDER. Shut the fuck up, you're followin' me this time.

Hayley gathers herself.

YOUNGER. As I was saying/

OLDER. I'm not fucking finished.

The church falls silent.

Look at you.

All of you.

Believing this fuck.

An' her lies.

Chloe stands up.

YOUNGER. Dad, please.

It's Nan's funeral.

OLDER. I know it is.

An' it's the perfect time.

For fucking honesty.

The wobbly priest walks to me.

YOUNGER. Son, this is not the time.

OLDER. I push him aside and approach the alter.

(Slight pause.)

Now, Hayley.

The love of my life.

Would you mind?

Tellin' everyone what you did that night.

YOUNGER. You're sick, Jim.

You need to get help.

OLDER. That's not what I fuckin' asked.

YOUNGER. Think of your mother, Jim.

OLDER. My mother, think of her?

She died thinking I was an animal.

A fucking monster.

An' you.

You're the one that made her think that.

An' for what, for FUCKIN' what?

I lose it.

I run for her.

Passed my Ma's coffin an' straight for her.

She runs.

Down, around the alter.

Back passed my Ma.

I gain on her.

An' just as I jump for her.

She dodges.

YOUNGER. NO!

> *(Slight pause.)*

OLDER. I hit the coffin.

It falls.

Crashin' to the earth.

Hayley runs in to Chloe's arms.

An' I stop.

> *(Slight pause.)*

Heart thumpin'.

Silence.

I look around.

Larry, Steo.

Faces. All starin'.

Tears, flowin' down Chloe's face.

Hayley, motionless.

> *(Slight pause.)*

Chloe, I/

I'm grabbed.

Stopped.

NO!

Please.

Let me go.

I'm not the animal.

She is.

She's the one.

Get her.

Pull her out.

Please stop.

I'm pushed to the ground.

Starin' at the angels on the ceiling.

I loved you. I loved you. I love you.

(Lights begin glitch.)

YOUNGER. Get up.

OLDER. Get up.

YOUNGER. Get up.

OLDER. Get up.

YOUNGER. Get up.

OLDER. And get the fuck/

(Snap. The lights shift. 2005.)

YOUNGER. What?

OLDER. Down to breakfast, sleepy head.

YOUNGER. Hayley always woke me like that.

Mostly.

When I did nothin' stupid the night before.

After nights out, you know?

OLDER. Will you be late?

YOUNGER. Only a couple of hours.

OLDER. Okay, love, enjoy.

YOUNGER. Then it's four a.m.

And you're convinced you're quiet.

A fucking ballerina coming in.

But from the pillow comes.

OLDER. Are you for fucking real?

YOUNGER. Ah, love, you waited up.

OLDER. You *woke* me up.

YOUNGER. You're a light sleeper.

OLDER. You rang the fucking bell.

YOUNGER. I forgot my keys.

> *(Slight pause.)*

Seein' as we're both up.

OLDER. Four minutes of passion?

YOUNGER. Better than three minutes of passion.

OLDER. Enjoy the couch.

> *(Slight pause.)*

YOUNGER. Joke's on her.

Our couch is fuckin' deadly.

> *(Slight pause.)*

The couch was a bit of a reoccurrence.

Me and Hayley.

Childhood sweethearts.

Same school an' all.

>   *(Slight pause.)*

First day of school.

My Ma brought me in.

Me and twenty other little eejits.

Unaware that we were about to serve a fourteen-year sentence.

Role call.

Your name in Irish all of a sudden.

Taught our response.

Anseo, A Mhuinteoir.

Assigned seats.

OLDER. James, you will be here.

>   With Hayley.

>   Hayley, James. James, Hayley.

>   *(Slight pause.)*

YOUNGER. Now, I don't remember much.

>   I was five.

>   But I remember these feelings.

>   Feelings I didn't understand.

>   In places I didn't understand.

>   It was Romeo meets Juliet.

>   It was Ross meets Rachel.

It was Danny meets Sandy.

I swear, there was a fucking light shining behind her.

Outlining her silhouette.

An' it wasn't the sun, 'cause it never shines in Dublin.

I was speechless.

And I'll never forget the first thing she said to me.

    (Slight pause.)

OLDER. Sir, this bleedin' weirdo's gawkin' at me.

YOUNGER. She always had a way with words.

An' we never looked back.

Well, I didn't.

She wouldn't talk to me.

I'd play these little tricks on her, you know?

OLDER. Sir, my book is missing.

YOUNGER. Flirtin'.

OLDER. Sir, my bag is inside out.

YOUNGER. Just little things.

OLDER. Sir, there's chewing gum in me hair.

YOUNGER. She had to have her head shaved.

Now, looking back.

I was actually, in fact, bullying her.

I didn't mean anything.

It's just what I thought you did.

I never got that saying.

"Treat them mean."

But it's what I saw.

(Snap.)

OLDER. What did I fucking tell ya?

YOUNGER. An' at that age.

OLDER. Me dinner on the fuckin' table.

YOUNGER. You take that in.

OLDER. When I get home!

YOUNGER. Think it's how you act.

(Snap.)

But one night.

My Ma was watching a film.

I heard the music down the hall.

Stuck my head in, asked could I join.

OLDER. Of course, Darling.

YOUNGER. Watching them two.

OLDER. It doesn't matter if you win or lose, it's what you
do with your dancin' shoes.

YOUNGER. What's that mean, Ma?

OLDER. It means you keep going, you keep keeping on.

(Slight pause.)

YOUNGER. Watchin' them, I realised, it's not all like my
parents.

OLDER. *You're the one that I want.*

YOUNGER. Couples can be happy.

An' violence.

Isn't the route.

I held my Ma's hand.

An' we watched it all.

An' as it ended.

You are the one I want/

OLDER. Is there anyone fucking home?

YOUNGER. He was back.

OLDER. I enjoyed this, love.

YOUNGER. An' she went out to him.

OLDER. Ah, there you fucking are.

YOUNGER. I watched Danny and Sandy fly off.

OLDER. An' no fucking dinner.

YOUNGER. An' leave us behind.

OLDER. Fucking disgraceful.

　　　　(Slight pause.)

YOUNGER. It was always her. Never me.

　　I never understood it.

　　At that age.

　　What I did know.

　　Was that I'd never be like him.

　　The slaggin' stopped.

　　The bullyin' stopped.

　　Seven-year-old me.

　　A romantic over night.

　　I walked in the next mornin'.

　　Straight up to Hayley.

　　As she drank her morning carton of milk.

　　An' in front of the whole class.

Hayley Rourke.

I know you don't know me.

An' I know I don't know you.

But I just want you to know.

That I will always honour you.

I will never disrespect you.

An' will forever cherish you.

I love you.

You are the one I want.

Oh, oh, oh, Honey.

>   *(Slight pause.)*

Silence fell over morning milk.

Kids not knowing where to look.

Not knowing what they just saw.

Unable to process the levels of fucking romance they'd just witnessed.

The reaction, not what I expected.

OLDER. Hahahahahaha!

YOUNGER. Laughter.

Fucking laughter.

Did they laugh at Romeo?

Did they laugh at Ross?

Did they laugh at Danny?

No, they didn't.

Hayley went red.

Bright fuckin' red.

Scarlet.

Start bawlin'.

An' pegged it out of the room.

OLDER. Hayley, he loves ya!

YOUNGER. I did.

OLDER. He wants to marry ya.

YOUNGER. I did.

OLDER. State of him.

YOUNGER. Bit harsh from a seven year old.

At the time.

I didn't understand it all fully.

But I knew.

In my tiny skull that something happened.

That was the start of all that.

And what I wanted.

With her.

Love, marriage and kids.

I was very deep thinkin' fucking' seven year old, I tell ya'.

> *(Slight pause.)*

But as you grow. Other things happen.

OLDER. Miss, think I shit meself.

YOUNGER. New scandals replace yours.

Secondary school.

OLDER. Welcome students.

YOUNGER. Now, if you thought I was full on at seven.

In secondary.

A teenager

With hormones?

I was fucked.

Like most lads.

I was awkward.

Growin' in to my body.

All limbs.

OLDER. What's the story with your teeth?

YOUNGER. I'm growin' in to them/

OLDER. What's the craic with your head?

YOUNGER. I'm growin' in to it.

With my mallagh head.

Giant teeth.

An' pepperoni complexion.

I kept to myself.

Hayley?

Just got more beautiful.

All the lads were mad for her.

But none had the balls to talk to her.

I heard someone say that beautiful girls are the loneliest.

'Cause everyone thinks they're out of their league.

So they never talk to them.

Could be true.

Could be bollocks.

An' I'm fucked if I was going to find out.

I'd have walked up to her.

    (Snap.)

OLDER. Heya, Jim.

YOUNGER. Huh. *(Deep longing exhale.)*

    (Snap.)

Not going to happen.

Fuck that.

By the end of sixth year.

I grew into me teeth.

Grew into me head.

An' all me limbs.

OLDER. Here, you going to Steo's leaving party?

YOUNGER. The end of school.

OLDER. Going to be class.

YOUNGER. Everyone was going.

OLDER. Everyone's going.

YOUNGER. To try get the ride.

OLDER. You'll defo get the ride.

YOUNGER. Hopefully I'm invited.

OLDER. Here, you're not invited.

YOUNGER. What, why?

OLDER. Can't have virgins leggin' it 'round the gaf.

YOUNGER. The fuck's that even mean?

OLDER. Show up an' you're fucking dead.

YOUNGER. Grand.

> I headed home from school.

> Ragin'.

> Bored in my room.

> Night of the party.

> An' I can't go.

> 'Cause I'm a virgin?

> What the fuck?

> Given, I am.

> But still.

OLDER. Let's see how you fuckin' do/

YOUNGER. Commotion downstairs.

OLDER. Just you an' your precious son.

YOUNGER. As I hit the bottom of the stairs.

OLDER. Two useless cunts.

YOUNGER. He's at the door.

OLDER. Spongers.

YOUNGER. Locked.

OLDER. Should have done this years ago.

YOUNGER. Swayin'.

OLDER. Get out!

YOUNGER. An' she throws his bag at him.

> He doesn't like that.

OLDER. Fuckin' slut.

YOUNGER. He catches her across the face.

OLDER. You deserved that.

YOUNGER. I run. Grab him.

OLDER. Ah, the lil' bastard shows.

YOUNGER. I pin him to the wall.

OLDER. Get your fucking hands off me.

YOUNGER. I leather him.

OLDER. Me fuckin' jaw.

YOUNGER. An' it shakes him.

OLDER. Best of luck without me.

YOUNGER. As he stumbles towards the door.

OLDER. You haven't a hope.

YOUNGER. We'll be grand.

OLDER. We'll see, all she's good for is whorin' herself.

YOUNGER. Fuck you.

OLDER. Don't even think I'm your real Da.

YOUNGER. Thank God.

OLDER. Could be anyone from this estate.

YOUNGER. I hope you die alone.

OLDER. Don't worry, you will too.

Any man close to her will.

YOUNGER. An' he's gone.

Fallin' down the road.

An' I never saw him again.

I turn an' go to the sitting room.

She sits on the couch.

Tears running down her face.

Ma?

OLDER. Yes, son?

YOUNGER. All that he said.

OLDER. You don't believe that/

YOUNGER. Not for a second.

>   *(Slight pause.)*

Want to watch *Grease*?

OLDER. No, thanks, son.

YOUNGER. Okay.

OLDER. Stephen's Mam said there's a party tonight?

YOUNGER. Yeah.

OLDER. The end of your exams.

YOUNGER. Yeah.

OLDER. Are you not going?

YOUNGER. Was thinkin' I'd stay here with you.

OLDER. I'm fine. Go. Have fun. Be young.

YOUNGER. Okay, Ma.

As I leave.

OLDER. James?

YOUNGER. Yeah?

OLDER. Promise me something.

YOUNGER. Anything.

OLDER. Never be like your father.

YOUNGER. I won't.

OLDER. Promise me.

YOUNGER. I promise.

OLDER. I believe you.

Now go have fun.

YOUNGER. She is some woman, my Ma.

Outlasted that bastard.

An' got her freedom.

An' me?

I'd never be like him.

I'd make sure of it.

(Slight pause.)

Steo's party wasn't far.

Couple of roads over.

I get there.

Packed.

Say whatever you want about Steo.

He was a prick.

But he was a popular prick.

Probably 'cause he had abs.

Moths loves abs.

Story with that?

Suppose, moths love abs, fellas love tits.

You'll over look a lot if they've a good set of either.

Approach the front door.

I slide down the side.

Into the garden.

And blend in with the crowd.

Fellas, moths.

Drinking, dancing.

After the day I've had.

I need a beer.

I moved through the crowd.

Kitchen.

Open the fridge.

Hand on a beer.

Followed by a hand on my shoulder.

OLDER. They're my fucking beers, virgin.

YOUNGER. What's with this fella and virgins?

OLDER. What did I say?

YOUNGER. I'll go.

OLDER. What's the rush?

YOUNGER. He picks up my beer.

OLDER. You wanted a beer, didn't you?

YOUNGER. Come on, Steo.

He steps closer.

An' closer.

Holds the bottle high.

Everyone watchin' on.

Anticipation sweeps the room.

OLDER. Enjoy it, virgin.

YOUNGER. As he pulls back.

I close my eyes.

Followed by/

OLDER. Why are you being such a cunt, Steo?

YOUNGER. Hayley.

Grabs it off him.

OLDER. An' virgin?

The closest you've come to a vagina is your Ma's, when you crawled out.

YOUNGER. Brutal.

OLDER. So take your little dairylea dunker, an' fuck off.

YOUNGER. The room erupts.

Hayley walks over to me.

OLDER. You right, virgin?

YOUNGER. Yep.

She didn't give a fuck.

Grabbed some beers.

In front of Steo.

An' just strolled out.

> (*Slight pause.*)

See ya', Steo. Thanks for havin' us.

And we left. At first.

I didn't know what to say.

We just walked the estate.

Drinkin' Steo's beers.

Shocked.

Delighted.

This is Hayley Rourke.

If seven year old me could've seen this.

I'd have been a God to him/

OLDER. So, are you still in love with me then?

YOUNGER. Me heart dropped through me arse.

(Slight pause.)

OLDER. Well, are you?

YOUNGER. I was.

Of course I was.

But me bollocks if I was going to tell her.

(Slight pause.)

OLDER. No?

YOUNGER. Ah, that was years ago, Hayley.

OLDER. Grown up now, have ya'?

YOUNGER. I have.

OLDER. Grew in to those teeth too.

YOUNGER. Appreciate it.

OLDER. An' your head. An' your limbs.

YOUNGER. Again, appreciate it.

OLDER. No wonder I bawled my eyes out.

When you said you loved me.

YOUNGER. Don't blame ya.

Sorry 'bout that, by the way.

I just watched *Grease* for the first time.

OLDER. Wanted to be Danny, did you?

YOUNGER. Yeah, but I forgot one thing.

OLDER. What?

YOUNGER. I live in Ireland.

Where acts of spontaneous romance are met with fucking cringe.

(Snap.)

OLDER. Anyway, it's grand, it didn't upset me or an'thin'.

>*(Snap.)*

Yeah, seems it.

Still want to be Danny?

YOUNGER. Now? Nah, that was years ago.

OLDER. That's a pity.

YOUNGER. She leans in to my ear.

OLDER. Always thought of myself as a bit of a Sandy.

YOUNGER. Now, I'd to muster up every fiber of my being not go, *"Huuuuuh" (Deep longing exhale.)*

But I recovered.

An' followed it with.

I think I'll always be Danny.

She smiled.

An' then heaven an' earth collided.

An' the angels sang.

Because she kissed me.

Yep.

She. Kissed. Me.

I didn't have the whole.

Do I kiss her?

Does she want me to kiss her?

Will she deck me if I kiss her?

Nope. None of that.

She just lobbed the gob.

An' it was perfect.

Absolutely perfect.

(Slight pause.)

OLDER. Is that a boner?

YOUNGER. Almost perfect.

OLDER. I'll take that as a compliment.

YOUNGER. An' that was us.

I did shit in the leaving.

She did well.

Women are always smarter, aren't they?

We're thick fucks.

I got a trade.

An' she became an accountant.

Young love.

Smitten.

An' not just me.

Both of us.

We were that annoyin' couple.

Did everything together.

Got a little apartment.

Married young.

Worked hard.

And played hard.

Never too hard.

But one night.

That changed.

An' with it.

I did too.

(Slight pause.)

OLDER. New Year's party, Jim.

YOUNGER. Ah, Hayley, why?

OLDER. Why not?

YOUNGER. Just eejits usin' the gaf to get fucked.

OLDER. Come on, it'll be good.

YOUNGER. An' she leans in to my ear.

OLDER. I'll make it worth your while.

YOUNGER. Huh. *(Deep longing exhale.)*

OLDER. Good.

YOUNGER. An' I won't get too graphic.

But New Year's Eve.

I nearly put me back out.

Carnal.

Animal.

It was the best sex of my life.

So her New Year's party?

She could invite the fuckin' world.

Couldn't give a bollocks.

OLDER. Right, people are arriving.

YOUNGER. Brilliant.

Wall to wall people.

People I worked with.

People Hayley worked with.

Steo.

We grew up and became mates.

Funny aul' world.

Drinks, craic flowin'.

It was actually enjoyin' it.

Karaoke goin'/

> (**OLDER** *sings a line from 'Like A Virgin' by Madonna.*)

Go on, Steo.

OLDER. We're up.

YOUNGER. We are?

OLDER. Yep.

> (**YOUNGER & OLDER** *each sing a line from 'Summer Nights' from* Grease.*)

YOUNGER. Oh, well, oh, well, oh, well, oh/

OLDER. Five.

YOUNGER. Four.

OLDER. Three.

YOUNGER. Two.

OLDER. One.

YOUNGER. Happy New Year!

OLDER. Happy New Year!

YOUNGER. We kissed an' Auld Lang Syne blares.

An' we held each other, kissed and laughed.

It was perfect.

> (*Slight pause.*)

An' as the night ran on.

People ran off.

Winding down.

An' I copped, hadn't seen Hayley in a while.

So I went lookin'.

An' as I entered our bedroom.

There she was, with her friend Larry, Steo and a few others.

OLDER. Baby, I was going to get you.

YOUNGER. What's going on?

OLDER. Want a bump?

YOUNGER. They had lines on the bedside locker.

I walked over.

I'd never actually seen coke in person before.

OLDER. It's just to keep the party going, Baby.

YOUNGER. Em/

OLDER. Come on, you'll love it.

            (Slight pause.)

YOUNGER. Alright.

I'm handed a tenner.

An' I snort it.

Now, the minute it hit my skull.

It had me.

It raised me.

Played me.

Owned me.

My mind scrambled.

I felt...good.

Great.

Fucking amazing.

An' this...voice.

Emerged.

OLDER. Good fucking man.

YOUNGER. Ringing off.

OLDER. One is good.

YOUNGER. Sounding off.

OLDER. Two is better.

YOUNGER. At first I was thrown.

An' just ran with it.

Right, this is what being fucked sounds like.

But the next time I tried it.

OLDER. You're back.

YOUNGER. Would sound again.

OLDER. We're going to be good friends.

You and I.

YOUNGER. We all have a voice in our heads.

All of us.

But this was different.

It was forward.

Confident.

Made me feel good.

An' after my first bump.

It was every weekend.

Every single weekend.

Me, Steo, Hayley.

An' Larry would sort it for us.

He sold it.

An' he fucking loved us.

Why wouldn't he?

Years of parties.

Years of sessions.

Years of sleepless weekends.

Shite talk in kitchens.

OLDER. I'm tellin' ya'.

Spice Girls will never break up.

YOUNGER. Not sure, seems like there's tension there.

OLDER. Do you ever listen to the wind?

I mean, *really* listen to it.

YOUNGER. Can't say I have.

OLDER. I can get a full pack of Tayto up me arse without it poppin', watch.

YOUNGER. Right, I'm off.

Rollover after rollover.

And with me.

Every step of the way.

Was him.

And as he grew ever present.

Hayley began to fade back.

(*Slight pause.*)

Hayley, Baby.

Got us a bag.

OLDER. Don't want any.

YOUNGER. What, why?

OLDER. 'Cause it's all we're doing.

YOUNGER. No we're not.

OLDER. You shouldn't have a dealer on speed dial.

YOUNGER. He's speed dial number two.

OLDER. See.

YOUNGER. You're number one.

OLDER. I'm done.

(Slight pause.)

YOUNGER. I kept going.

OLDER. Her loss, man.

More for us.

YOUNGER. Yeah, more for us.

OLDER. An' she'll be back.

YOUNGER. Yeah, she'll be back.

OLDER. You'll always have me.

(Slight pause.)

YOUNGER. An' it was me an' him.

Others falling away.

Hayley.

Steo.

A mate we made called Pisa.

OLDER. 'Cause I'm always leanin', man.

YOUNGER. Eh, cool.

    They all fell away.

    Just me.

OLDER. An' me.

    I'll never leave ya.

        (Slight pause.)

YOUNGER. One evening, dropped into Larry.

    Lane way, off Grafton.

    Black door.

    He'd buzz you in.

OLDER. Come on up, brother.

YOUNGER. As always, I did.

    Every Monday to get me through the week.

    An' every Friday to get me through the weekend.

    Hug.

    Story.

    Usual.

        (Slight pause.)

OLDER. Here, listen. Need a chat.

YOUNGER. Go for it.

OLDER. Hayley was in.

YOUNGER. For her own bag?

OLDER. No, the opposite.

    She told me to cut you off.

YOUNGER. Sake. Cut me off.

    She's the one that started me.

OLDER. Listen, I'm not gettin' involved.

YOUNGER. Are you cuttin' me off?

OLDER. Wouldn't be a very good coke dealer if I did, would I?

YOUNGER. Good man.

OLDER. But if she catches you, you got it elsewhere.

YOUNGER. An' if she comes back to you.

OLDER. You got it elsewhere.

YOUNGER. Exactly.

   As I return home.

OLDER. We need to talk.

YOUNGER. What's up?

OLDER. You need to get off that shit.

YOUNGER. What shit?

OLDER. You're on it most days.

   I can see it.

YOUNGER. I'm not/

OLDER. I said get the fuck off it.

YOUNGER. Interesting.

   'Cause you're the one that got me on it.

   I did this for you.

   You loved to do it.

OLDER. When we were younger, Jim.

   Trying things.

   You're in your thirties.

YOUNGER. Barely.

OLDER. Listen, just drop it.

I spoke to Larry.

YOUNGER. As she speaks.

My friend starts to echo.

Down the back of my skull.

OLDER. The fucking cheek of this one.

YOUNGER. Growing.

OLDER. She needs to take it down a peg.

YOUNGER. Growing.

OLDER. An' shut her fucking mouth.

YOUNGER. I haven't seen Larry in a while.

OLDER. I know you were there.

So whatever's in your pocket.

Give me it.

YOUNGER. Excuse me?

OLDER. Give it to me now.

YOUNGER. There's nothing to give.

OLDER. Now!

YOUNGER. I've nothing.

OLDER. Fucking now!

(Slight pause.)

Now!

Before I really start.

(Slight pause.)

YOUNGER. I'll get rid of it.

OLDER. Down the toilet, please.

YOUNGER. I walk in to the toilet.

   Open the bag.

OLDER. Can't believe you're listening to her.

YOUNGER. I do a bump.

OLDER. That's more like it.

YOUNGER. An' flush it down.

OLDER. Fuckin' loser.

YOUNGER. I call her in.

   Let her see it.

OLDER. Good. I'm proud of you.

YOUNGER. Thanks, Baby.

OLDER. I'll get you some tampons next.

   Fuckin' hell.

YOUNGER. I ignore him.

   (Slight pause.)

OLDER. You know I love you.

YOUNGER. I love you too.

OLDER. Those days are gone.

   And we've much brighter days ahead.

YOUNGER. We do.

OLDER. You can do this.

   For me.

YOUNGER. For you.

   (Slight pause.)

OLDER. Now, I've something to tell you.

　　The reason I want you off it.

　　　　(Slight pause.)

　　I'm pregnant.

YOUNGER. With a baby?

OLDER. With a baby, you dope.

　　　　(Slight pause.)

YOUNGER. What, really? Holy shit.

OLDER. We're going to have a baby.

YOUNGER. We're going to have a baby.

　　　　(Slight pause.)

　　We hug.

　　We cry.

　　We smile.

OLDER. So lay off that shit.

　　For me.

　　For the baby.

YOUNGER. I promise.

　　　　(Slight pause.)

　　Jesus.

OLDER. Don't worry.

　　We'll keep it goin'.

　　Babies are hyper.

　　We'll be hyper.

YOUNGER. I ignore him.

(Slight pause.)

As the pregnancy went on.

I tried.

I really did.

But every time I went out.

OLDER. Let's step it up a notch.

YOUNGER. An' I listened.

Couldn't stop.

Couldn't turn away.

Yep, gimme that.

Gimme all o'that.

I kept using.

But I'll stop when the baby's here.

Larry kept his mouth shut.

An' she knew nothing.

(Slight pause.)

One night.

A Saturday.

There I was.

She's resting.

OLDER. What's a couple of bumps going to hurt?

YOUNGER. Now?

OLDER. Now's always good.

YOUNGER. One bump.

OLDER. Two bumps.

YOUNGER. Three bumps.

OLDER. Four bumps.

YOUNGER. More than I should.

    On watch.

    She's due to pop any day.

    But it won't be tonight.

    Big fat line.

    Bliss.

        (Pause.)

OLDER. Get this fucking baby out of me.

YOUNGER. We had done everything to help it along.

    Spicy food. They say that helps.

    Made her an Indian.

    I blew the bollocks off her.

    She cried.

    Had the shits for three hours.

    But still no joy.

    An' tonight. Sex.

    We gave that a go.

    You go on top.

OLDER. With all these chins, fuck off.

YOUNGER. Okay, I will.

OLDER. An' not know what you're doing behind me bump.

YOUNGER. Then what?

OLDER. Get behind me.

YOUNGER. Behind you.

OLDER. Yes. Lie there and I'll move in.

YOUNGER. This is so sexy.

OLDER. Shut up. This is your fault.

YOUNGER. I lie there.

　　And she backs in.

OLDER. Here I go.

YOUNGER. Like I'm guiding her in to a parking spot.

OLDER. Here I come.

YOUNGER. Beep, beep, beep, beep/

OLDER. Prick.

YOUNGER. Up she gets.

OLDER. I could kill you.

YOUNGER. Relax.

　　　　(Pause.)

OLDER. What did you just say?

YOUNGER. Relax.

　　　　(Slight pause.)

OLDER. Relax?

　　Relax?

　　Fucking relax?

　　FUCKING RELAX?

YOUNGER. I remember someone, somewhere.

　　Tellin' me, never to tell a woman to relax.

　　It's like setting off a nuclear bomb.

　　Add pregnancy to that?

　　This was fucking Hiroshima.

She blew.

OLDER. FUCKING RELAX!

Oh!

YOUNGER. What?

OLDER. Me water just broke.

YOUNGER. I look down.

It has.

I'll get the mop/

OLDER. Get the fucking keys.

Get the bag.

You fucking eejt.

YOUNGER. Now?

OLDER. Yes, now!

YOUNGER. Fuck.

Maybe we'll get an ambulance.

Be quicker.

OLDER. Jim, get the fucking keys.

YOUNGER. Hayley shouts.

I do.

An' we're in to the car.

OLDER. We can do it.

YOUNGER. I can't drive like this.

OLDER. We can do it, man.

YOUNGER. Ready?

OLDER. Drive!

YOUNGER. I step on it.

High as a fuckin' kite.

Bombing it in to The Coombe.

Down the Crumlin Road.

OLDER. Red light, Jim.

YOUNGER. Fuck it.

I'm getting that baby out of you/

OLDER. Slow down/

YOUNGER. Not a chance.

I was on it.

Heightened.

Tunnel vision.

OLDER. Jim!

YOUNGER. We're nearly there.

OLDER. You're going to fucking kill us.

Jim!

YOUNGER. I skid in to the car park and stop.

Made it.

Let's get me heir out of you.

(*Slight pause.*)

OLDER. Look at me.

YOUNGER. What?

OLDER. Fucking look at me.

YOUNGER. We have to get in, come on.

OLDER. You fucking prick.

YOUNGER. What?

OLDER. Look at your eyeballs.

YOUNGER. There's nothing wrong with my eyeballs.

OLDER. You bastard.

YOUNGER. She loses it.

OLDER. BASTARD!

YOUNGER. I haven't done anything.

OLDER. Off your fucking head.

YOUNGER. I've never seen her like this.

She screams.

OLDER. Bastard.

YOUNGER. Shouts.

OLDER. Bastard.

YOUNGER. An' swings.

OLDER. Don't follow me.

YOUNGER. She catches me across the jaw.

An' heads in to the hospital.

(Slight pause.)

OLDER. That could've gone better.

YOUNGER. I'm a disgrace.

OLDER. You got here, didn't you?

YOUNGER. That didn't feel like me.

OLDER. 'Cause it was me.

Now grow a set an' get in there.

YOUNGER. I grab a coffee.

An' find out where she is.

When I find her.

OLDER. Help me!

YOUNGER. She's in labour.

OLDER. Jim/

YOUNGER. I'm here.

OLDER. Oh God!

YOUNGER. It's okay.

I'm here.

Push.

Push.

Push.

OLDER. AAAAAAAH!

(Slight pause.)

YOUNGER. Holy shit.

(Slight pause.)

I'm handed this little ball of mush.

Holy fuck.

I wept. Instantly.

She was just...perfect.

OLDER. Do we have a name?

YOUNGER. We do.

Chloe.

Hey, lil' nugget.

I'm your Da.

I'll never let anyone hurt you.

An' I won't be telling you you've a vagina until you're thirty.

Have to say.

The day she was born.

Hands down.

Best day of my life.

When Hayley came to.

OLDER. You need to go get help, Jim.

I mean it.

Or you're gone.

YOUNGER. I don't say anything.

I just nod.

OLDER. I mean it.

> *(Pause.)*

YOUNGER. In the months that followed

I kept a lid on it.

Even tried a couple of meetings.

I took a week off.

To care for Chloe.

When Hayley went back to work.

It was my first time, on my own with Chloe.

OLDER. If you need anything.

Ring me.

YOUNGER. Don't worry, we'll be fine.

> *(Slight pause.)*

And we were.

For a little bit.

Fed her, changed her and put her down.

A few hours pass.

She'd sleep for hours.

So I did a few lines.

No problem in that.

She was safe and sound.

And I wanted to take the edge off.

OLDER. Good shout, she's asleep.

YOUNGER. Yeah, exactly.

Before I knew where I was.

A bag was gone.

OLDER. Get another.

YOUNGER. Just a bump or two out of it.

Take out another.

And before I know, that's gone too.

Then/

OLDER. Fuck.

YOUNGER. Chloe.

OLDER. Jaysus, that's deafening.

YOUNGER. I run in.

Pick her up.

Fed her.

But she won't stop.

OLDER. Is she alright?

YOUNGER. She's grand.

Fuck off an' leave me with her.

(Slight pause.)

She won't stop.

Crying, crying, crying.

I try everything.

I need a bump.

I put her down, she wailes.

I have to pick her up, fuck.

Come on, darling.

Just stop for one second.

And Daddy will pick you up.

No joy.

Screams, piercing my skull.

I have her on my lap.

I take out the bag.

And put it on her blanket.

Just one, Baby.

And I'll hold you all day.

I snort it up an'/

OLDER. What the fuck are you doing?

YOUNGER. Hayley, in the doorway, home.

She, she wouldn't stop crying.

OLDER. Give me my child.

YOUNGER. She takes Chloe off me.

Let me explain.

OLDER. Get out.

YOUNGER. Hayley/

OLDER. Get out or I call the guards.

YOUNGER. Hayley/

OLDER. Now.

(Slight pause.)

YOUNGER. I'll be back later.

OLDER. I don't want you back.

YOUNGER. I'll be back later.

(Slight pause.)

I wasn't back later.

I went on the rip.

For a few days, I think.

A few mates I knew.

Couch hopped.

Partied.

My idea was that I needed to let it out.

Get it out of my system.

An' I could go home.

I loved them too much.

And I'd never leave them, never.

So when the drugs were gone.

I went home.

About ten.

The gaf in darkness.

When I got there.

My key wouldn't work.

Locks changed.

What the fuck?

I called out.

Circled the house.

Hayley!

Hayley!

Fuck this.

I go to the back door.

Smash the window.

In I climb.

As I get in, I trip, fall and no/

Fall towards the sitting room.

Trying to stop myself.

But no, head over heels.

Through the coffee table.

Glass smashes.

Fuck.

    (Slight pause.)

After a moment.

OLDER. I told you I wanted you gone.

YOUNGER. Hayley, I'm sorry.

OLDER. Get out of my house.

YOUNGER. Your house? I live here too.

OLDER. Get out, please.

YOUNGER. Changing the locks, nice one.

OLDER. James, you need to leave us.

You need to get help. You haven't been going to your meetings.

YOUNGER. I get to my feet.

Hayley, darling.

I love you.

OLDER. I love you too but we can't live like this.

YOUNGER. It can get better.

OLDER. No, it can't. It's only getting worse.

YOUNGER. I can make it better.

OLDER. Please, leave us.

YOUNGER. When are you going to realise?

I'll never leave you.

You're my girls.

OLDER. Good night, Jim.

YOUNGER. And she walks up the stairs.

(Pause.)

I think she accepted it.

I've loved Hayley my whole life.

An' I'm going to love her my whole life.

Over the next few weeks.

Things were tough.

She retreated.

We spoke, sparingly.

I knew I could get it right.

And I haven't touched anything.

Since that night.

Few months later.

The christening.

Everyone came out.

Fuckers I hadn't seen in years.

Hayley weeps.

My Ma weeps.

I fucking weep.

Steo, godfather.

The party?

Let's do it.

Before we left.

I won't be touching anything.

OLDER. No?

YOUNGER. No.

OLDER. Good for you, James.

YOUNGER. I'll just be having a few drinks.

OLDER. Just a few drinks.

YOUNGER. Nothing more.

(*Slight pause.*)

I'd been doing well.

OLDER. Come on, man.

YOUNGER. Ignoring him.

OLDER. Listen to me.

YOUNGER. Pushing him further back.

OLDER. Fucking benny, you'd do anything she says.

YOUNGER. The baby's head is soaked.

We go to the Garda Club.

There's a homeless fella outside.

OLDER. Any change?

YOUNGER. Now, I was highly strung.

   The stress of the day.

   No, I fucking don't.

OLDER. Alright, was only askin'/

YOUNGER. That's all you are ever doin', askin'.

   Fucking homeless.

   In I go.

   There are two rooms.

   One up.

   One down.

   Inside the door/

OLDER. Jaysus, Jim.

YOUNGER. Howya, Larry.

OLDER. What has ya' here?

YOUNGER. The little one's christening.

OLDER. Ah, beautiful, beautiful. Just beautiful.

YOUNGER. Hayley sees him. I think she's going to kick off.

OLDER. Pop in later, Larry, if you're about, say hello.

YOUNGER. That was weird.

   I go to the bar.

   I grab a drink an' sit with my Ma.

   Great day, isn't it?

OLDER. It's been a gorgeous day.

YOUNGER. That priest was a little wobbly, wasn't he?

OLDER. I thought Chloe was getting dropped in at one point.

YOUNGER. He'd be going in after her.

(*Slight pause.*)

OLDER. Hayley told me about a few things.

YOUNGER. About what?

OLDER. The fights.

The neighbours' complaints.

The drugs.

YOUNGER. I'm off it, Ma.

OLDER. Son, if you're not very careful.

You're going to lose it all.

YOUNGER. I won't lose anything, Ma.

OLDER. Hayley said, you can get aggressive.

YOUNGER. Sorry? I never get aggressive.

OLDER. That stuff changes you, Son.

YOUNGER. I never get aggressive.

OLDER. You probably don't even remember it.

YOUNGER. I remember everything.

OLDER. He's always there.

YOUNGER. Who is?

OLDER. Your father.

YOUNGER. I'm nothing like him.

OLDER. When I first met him.

He was charming, sweet, funny.

YOUNGER. I'm nothing like him.

OLDER. Then he slowly began to change.

YOUNGER. Listen to me/

OLDER. No, you listen to me.

> *(Slight pause.)*

He turned in to something else.

A different person.

The drink took him.

Molded him.

Twisted him.

In to what it wanted.

A monster.

It spoke to him.

YOUNGER. Spoke to him?

OLDER. Spoke to him.

Comforted him.

Led him.

YOUNGER. I hear you, Ma.

OLDER. Good.

Because I see it in you.

YOUNGER. I won't become him.

OLDER. You promised.

YOUNGER. She kisses me on the head.

An' goes to hold Chloe.

> *(Slight pause.)*

OLDER. What a load of bollocks.

YOUNGER. Shut up.

OLDER. You going to listen to that shite?

YOUNGER. She's right.

OLDER. Right, would you fuck off.

YOUNGER. No, you need to fuck off.

OLDER. All we do is have the craic.

YOUNGER. Not anymore.

OLDER. Are you seriously going to listen to this bollocks?

YOUNGER. I am.

OLDER. Wait.

>   *(Slight pause.)*

>   Jim, man. Wait/

>   *(Slight pause.)*

YOUNGER. I walk over to Hayley.

>   I'm sorry, love.

>   For everythin'.

>   *(Slight pause.)*

OLDER. It's okay, Jim. It's who you are.

YOUNGER. An' she goes to my Ma.

>   *(Slight pause.)*

>   Aggressive.

>   Where did that come from?

>   I've never.

>   An' will never.

>   Lay a hand on her.

The biggest fear.

Becoming like him.

    (Slight pause.)

An' I never will be.

    (Slight pause.)

The party continues.

The kids leave.

My Ma takes Chloe home.

OLDER. I'll see you tomorrow, Son.

Love you.

YOUNGER. Love you too, Ma.

    (Slight pause.)

An' the party gets loose.

Dancin'. Shots.

Cues for the cubicles.

When you know nobody's waitin' for a shite.

Doors closed.

Sniff goes.

I go in.

An' just go the jacks.

Nothin' more.

But with each visit.

Me mind wanders.

Twitches.

Leans towards the hit.

But I resist.

The night descends.

I go in to the jacks.

I look beside me.

Larry.

OLDER. Here, he has some.

C'mon.

Let us loose.

Alright, pal.

YOUNGER. You made it in.

OLDER. You're lookin' a bit glum.

YOUNGER. It's me baby's christenin'.

I'm flyin'.

OLDER. Well, this'll help you reach the sky.

YOUNGER. He pops a bag in my top pocket.

OLDER. On the house.

YOUNGER. An' he leaves.

(Slight pause.)

I stand, facin' the mirror.

OLDER. We're set.

YOUNGER. An' for the first time.

OLDER. Let's go.

YOUNGER. I see a face with the voice.

OLDER. Just you an' me.

YOUNGER. An' we both want the same thing.

OLDER. That's the job.

YOUNGER. I look at the bag.

Open it.

No.

OLDER. Excuse me?

YOUNGER. I don't want this shite.

OLDER. Yes, you do.

YOUNGER. An' I drop it down the sink.

OLDER. What the fuck are you doing?

YOUNGER. Fuck off, you.

(Pause.)

Then the door flies open.

OLDER. Here he is.

YOUNGER. Hayley.

OLDER. Couldn't resist, could you?

YOUNGER. I can explain.

OLDER. Explain nothin'/

YOUNGER. I can/

OLDER. You dirty junkie/

YOUNGER. I'm not a junkie.

OLDER. Oh yeah, you're not?

Then what's this?

YOUNGER. She rubs her hand on the bag.

OLDER. Take it!

YOUNGER. And smears it into my face.

OLDER. Off your face the last few years.

Every day.

In an' out.

Drivin' me, in labour, off the mallagh.

YOUNGER. I wasn't expectin' you to/

OLDER. Oh, I'm sorry.

Should've held it in.

YOUNGER. That's not what I/

OLDER. No matter how many times I threw you out.

You always came back.

YOUNGER. I love you.

I'll always come back.

OLDER. No matter how bad you make our lives.

YOUNGER. What?

OLDER. You always come back.

And always will.

YOUNGER. Always will.

It's me and my girls.

(*Slight pause.*)

OLDER. Not anymore.

YOUNGER. Hayley/

OLDER. You left me no choice.

YOUNGER. What do you mean?

OLDER. You'll never go.

You'll just make things worse and worse.

Me and Chloe.

We're not being prisoners.

YOUNGER. She turns to the mirror.

OLDER. This is to be rid of you.

YOUNGER. An' smacks her head down.

OLDER. Fuck/

YOUNGER. Bouncin' off the sink.

OLDER. Help!

YOUNGER. What are you doing?

OLDER. Help me, please!

YOUNGER. Crack again.

OLDER. He's gone mad.

YOUNGER. Hayley, what are you doing?

OLDER. What you did?

It was vile.

I don't want you near our baby.

But you just won't go.

I need you gone.

Forever.

YOUNGER. Her face opens as she hits the sink.

OLDER. You'll never see her again.

YOUNGER. She jumps on me.

Smearin' the blood all over me.

An' as the door flies open.

OLDER. Please, he's trying to kill me.

YOUNGER. They're shocked by the scene.

Everyone gets a look.

OLDER. Jim, what the fuck have you done?

YOUNGER. I protest.

I didn't do...

I didn't...

I swear.

The guards are called.

I fall to the ground.

> *(Lights begin glitch.)*

OLDER. Get up.

YOUNGER. Get up.

OLDER. Get up.

YOUNGER. Get up.

OLDER. Get up.

> *(The lights glitch and flash. Increasing in intensity. Past and present collide.)*

YOUNGER. The ceiling blurs.

OLDER. Starin' at the angels.

YOUNGER. The bathroom/

OLDER. The church.

YOUNGER. Voices crowd me.

OLDER. Surround me.

YOUNGER. Pinned/

OLDER. To the ground.

YOUNGER. Hayley/

OLDER. Stands over me.

YOUNGER. Blood/

OLDER. Tears/

TOGETHER. Rushing down her face.

YOUNGER. From the bathroom floor/

TOGETHER. My screams echo/

OLDER. Around the church.

YOUNGER. The aftermath.

OLDER. That night.

YOUNGER. There were so many questions.

OLDER. They had so many questions.

YOUNGER. Mr. Shaw, why did you attack your wife?

OLDER. I didn't attack her.

YOUNGER. She did that herself.

OLDER. Do you know how many times we've heard this story?

YOUNGER. You were covered in her blood.

OLDER. She was smashin' her head off the sink.

YOUNGER. And there are illegal drugs in your system/

OLDER. She fucking did that.

YOUNGER. I didn't take them.

OLDER. Please, lower your voice, Sir.

YOUNGER. We've complaints from your neighbours.

OLDER. Going back months.

YOUNGER. Your wife fearing for her life.

OLDER. Even your own mother has made a statement.

YOUNGER. What has she said?

OLDER. That there's a history of domestic violence in the family.

YOUNGER. My Da was abusive.

OLDER. And you witnessed it.

YOUNGER. I did.

OLDER. An' have done the same.

YOUNGER. I haven't turned out like him.

OLDER. I fucking promised!

YOUNGER. An' I kept that promise.

OLDER. I always will.

YOUNGER. I loved you.

OLDER. I loved you.

TOGETHER. I love you.

YOUNGER. How did I get here?

OLDER. How am I here!

YOUNGER. This isn't who I am.

OLDER. I'm a good man.

YOUNGER. I can do better/

OLDER. I can.

YOUNGER. I really can/

OLDER. The angels look down on me.

YOUNGER. Help me/

OLDER. Give me a chance.

YOUNGER. Please/

OLDER. Please!

YOUNGER. It doesn't matter if you win or lose.

OLDER. It's what you do with your dancin' shoes.

YOUNGER. Chloe/

OLDER. Ma/

YOUNGER. Hayley!

(Pause.)

TOGETHER. I'm sorry.

("Consolers of the Lonely" by The Raconteurs plays. Blackout.)

The End

www.ingramcontent.com/pod-product-compliance
Ingram Content Group UK Ltd.
Pitfield, Milton Keynes, MK11 3LW, UK
UKHW021517270725
461234UK00002B/24